I Only Left for Tea: Poems

I Only Left for Tea:
Poems

by

Al Black

I ONLY LEFT FOR TEA: POEMS. Copyright 2014 by Al Black. All rights reserved. Printed in the United States of America. No part of this book may be used or reproduced in any manner whatsoever without written permission except in the case of brief quotations in critical articles or reviews. Contact Muddy Ford Press, 1009 Muddy Ford Road, Chapin, SC 29036.

First edition.

Library of Congress Number : 2014947768

ISBN:978-1-942081-00-5

Cover art by Kevin Neireiter

Contents

Mixing Bowl   9

I

Shut the Door   13

Sometimes   14

Summer Solstice   15

Wild Raspberry Stains   16

Old Photo of Bob, with His Mother   18

Thinking of Dan   19

Daydream   21

Lessons I Learned in Church   22

Emily's Breast   24

When I Was Nine   26

Hot July   27

Tides   28

Bob Hinkle   29

It Lingers   31

Sometimes II   32

II

Edge of the Woods 33

Fog   36

Blue Tick Hound, or a Southern Tale   37

Gristle and Bone   38

Voyeur   39

His Hands   40

To the Girl Unknown   41

Daughter of Light   42

A Letter to Miss Harvey   43

Poem for a Friend Whose Lover Committed Suicide   44

A Generation of Mad Hatters   45

Exit 141   46

Blood   47

Estrangement   48

Childhood Friends   49

Henry Miller   50

Herstory   51

Don't Call Me Jonah   52

III

I Only Left for Tea   55

Grandma's Cabinet   56

Pink Roses   57

Prefab Cracker Boxes   58

Signing With the Frogs   59

Stone Moss   60

Prometheus   61

Daybreak   62

Dim Light of Expectations   63

Questions I Ask of Spring   64

Alone   65

Three Poems for Others   66

Playing House   67

Walking the Banks   68

Summer Solstice II   69

Four Haiku   70

Winter Poem   71

Blankets   72

Weightless   73

Soon   74

Mixing Bowl

My kitchen has many ingredients;
Shall I serve you cake or gruel?
Run, go find a mixing bowl.

Cupboards and shelves filled with
Cream and vinegar — sugar and salt,
Run, go find a mixing bowl.

My heart has many emotions;
Help me choose a sweet recipe.
Run, go find a mixing bowl.

I

Shut the Door

One icy Sunday, the pastor preached of a loving God
Who cared even for the sparrow that falls
Later, at home my father said shut the garage door
A storm is coming
Outside, backs to the wind
Birds huddled on the power lines
I worried how would they survive?
I left the garage door open a bit

After the storm
Father found the garage door was not closed
No explanation was asked for
None was given
God may care for the fallen sparrow
But he does not care for little boys
Who dicker in God's business
And then cry themselves to sleep

I took my beating like a man.

Sometimes

Sometimes, my mom would sit me down
Next to a stack of ironing
She would go over language lessons while
Pressing out imperfections and wrinkles
This was my pre-school education
Her gift of time
A luxury she never had as a child
She was the eldest of many
So bright — so young — so trapped
With chores to do and piles and piles of ironing

Where did her time go?
Now, her hair is so thin and white
Brittle from gallons of hair spray
Applied every Sunday morning
Before my father would drop her off early
At the back door of the church
Her dress always pressed just right under her choir robe
Every hair on her head would sit perfectly quiet in its place
Evidence to all of her propriety and godly living
While her children would squirm restlessly in a pew
Waiting for their father to shut his eyes during the sermon
So they could play tic-tac-toe

Summer Solstice

Racing the sun
Hot air — no wind
Dust trail like a tracer bullet
Hung behind our car
Pointing to our hiding place

Too young to worry about dying
We went skinny–dipping in the creek
No past — no future — only now

Wild Raspberry Stains

I remember picking wild raspberries
In the woods behind the fairgrounds
Stealing time from obligations
And trying to figure out how a bear
Could grow so big and frightful
Always in the woods stealing honey
Foraging for berries
And sleeping in all winter

Growing up in a large religious family
Every freedom — every delight
Had a cost attached to it
But in the woods I was free
No rules, no chores
No one making fun of second-hand clothes
I would disappear for hours
Just careful to be home on time

So there I was picking raspberries
With purple fingers and lips
Thinking about the bear and
Knowing I was late
Knowing I had a whopping coming
My rear end would look like my t-shirt
All purple splotches

Then again, what did it matter
I'd have to pay the price anyway
So I kept on picking and eating
Looking over my shoulder
For that big old angry bear
And wondering what it would be like
To come from a small family
That did not go to church

Old Photo of Bob, with His Mother

Head high, — chin in hand
Bright red confidence
In her kitchen she knows
She is her own woman

Straw-hatted boy
Bends into her space
He knows who he is
He is his momma's boy

Thinking of Dan

Sunrise, walking the streets of the French Quarter
New Orleans yawns, stretches and welcomes the end
      of night
I walk towards the river and Cafe du Monde
Where the Cathedral of St. Louis sits
On her throne overlooking Jackson Square

Near the river a bench is calling my name
I will relax, observe and write about the birthplace of jazz
Perched like a pigeon on the roof of a church
I open my notebook and watch the sun rise over the city

"Are you writing your masterpiece?"
Surprised at his gap-toothed grin — I smile
"No, just writing my musings"
He smiles again
"I used to write"
Another gap-toothed grin, apprehensive, trying to be
      friendly
"You know Anne Rice visits here sometimes"
Is he looking for intelligent conversation?
"She has an apartment nearby"
Or a connection back to the world he once knew
"I painted it once, she writes there"
He smiles his best gap-toothed grin, again
"I can take you there"

His smile leaves — he turns — he walks away
I want to cry out
"Sit with me and tell me what you have written"
But I am afraid not of him — I am afraid of me
My shadow self — my insistent self — the me that haunts
      my nightmares

That wants to live in alleys, step into oblivion
Dance to my addictions
But I have my responsibilities, people who care about me
    and my notebooks
Anyway, he would probably abuse my kindness

He continues walking
I cannot look away
His friends, his people, call to him
Leather-skinned, scruffy, ill-fit clothes in need of an iron
"Ragamuffins" my mother would say
Sunken, hollow empty eyes waiting to be filled
Homeless, hobos, derelicts, vagabonds, addicts
Strippers, thieves, prostitutes, fathers, mothers, sons and
    daughters,
Wasted, gone, nothing to sell and nothing to use
I walk the other way, asking myself
Why do we have back alleys where we hide our rubbish
Once, they were dreamers, artists, musicians and poets
Full with music, laughter and love

Daydream

On a shelf preserving their youth
My parents' wedding picture sits
Her hat sat joyful as a Sunday amid her auburn hair
She wore a mint green dress
It was her wedding day

The war was over
Her prayers were answered
He returned on a winter's day
Alive with wavy red hair
He had come to take her away

Today, visiting my parents
I am sitting on their couch
Mom is dozing in her reading chair
Newspaper in her lap
Hair thin crisp and white as an angel's

Dad is on the other side of
The room snoring in his recliner
Dog in his lap
Head shining like a pale moon
TV droning — as they daydream of 1946

Lessons I Learned in Church

Sunday morning, sitting on the porch
Listening to an off-key choir of geese
My grass is high, irregular and lush
God created flowering weeds to stand beautiful in my yard
If my father would come by for a visit and see my lawn
He would huff and puff about the Sabbath Day being
       special
Demand to know what the hell I did on Saturday
Then turn to my mother and say,
"Come on, Alice, let's go."

My father has strong opinions about the days of the week
High on his list was that God created Saturday
So his true believers may prepare for Sunday
Growing up, come hell or high water
On Saturday, my father's children were true believers
Mow the lawn so the grass lays at just the right angle
Get a haircut downtown from Mr. Casto
Shine the shoes that you only wear on Sundays
Even though they were shined just last week
Press your Sunday dress pants and lay your Bible out for
       morning
After you had wasted the better part of Saturday
He expected you to stay home on Sunday
Something about the day of rest
I believed that if he left us alone on Saturday
We wouldn't need to rest on Sunday

I never took anything my father said as whole cloth,
Looking for tiny holes in the fabric, I had my quiet
    rebellion
Asking the barber to leave it just a fraction longer
Missing a small spot with polish on the heel of my shoe
Forgetting to trim the grass along the fence behind the
    garage
Wearing my Sunday dress pants without underwear

Until one Sunday, in ninth grade,
I had snuck away to make out with an eighth grade girl in
    the church library
Coming back I stopped in the bathroom
Hallelujah!! I am jumping up and down and speaking in
    tongues
I have zipped my ball sack in the zipper
Hallelujah!! I am jumping up and down and speaking in
    tongues
It hurt just as much zipping it back out
Bleeding like a stuck hog
No amount of toilet tissue could stop the flow

That Sunday, I learned why sanitary napkins are so thick
    and bulky
Why some folks must touch a hot stove to believe that it is
    hot
And why I will never again wear zippered pants without
    underwear

Emily's Breast

When I was nine we first met
You were sitting in my living room
On a shelf in the pages of a book
My mother kept from her childhood

Your verses spoke to me — saved me from suicide
Or homicide – or maybe both
You told me it was OK to have secrets
To be hurt, to be different

At fifteen I bought your collected works
The ones they found hidden in your room
Verses you left just for me
An invitation to come into your upstairs bedroom

We would lie naked
Your tongue covering me with moist desires
Like the wet ink you never dared write
We held each other tight

Murmuring private thoughts
I would beg you to elope with me
Kiss your upturned breast
. . . and leave before the morning light

I still read your love letters
Verses that only I understand
Verses that hint of betrayal
. . . of violation — of hope

I walk the leafy lanes of Amherst
. . . and peer up at your window
You part your curtain
Show me your alabaster breast

. . . and whisper "I'm OK"
"Are You?"

When I Was Nine

I am the positive one
I have coffee with friends
I listen
I give them hope
I help them go on living

Later, alone over cold coffee
I read Anne Sexton
She sees beneath my smile
She laughs at my pious faithfulness
She sticks her fingers in her genitalia
I lick her fingers and taste her depression

We lie naked
I tell her my dreams
The ones where I chase the man in the shiny car
Who threw me in the grass by the road
"Go home little boy, your mother is calling"
I want to catch him and kill the man
Statistics say I may become

I am the positive one
I have coffee with friends
I listen
I give them hope
I help them go on living
I pick the grass from their hair
I say, "Tell me your story"
For mine is too much to bear

Hot July

I wake alone
In a hot July dawn for prayers
I roll out of bed and reach
Back to touch your thigh
But you are not there

You are gone again
We just talk on the phone, send emails
And post photos and comments on Facebook
This morning, I sit here at my computer
Remembering that hot Sunday in July
When we first met after church
In the parking lot – you were only sixteen

Or the next year on that hot July night
When we slipped away to a motel
So we could spend a night alone
Not in the backseat of a '65 Impala
Hoping no one would catch us
You kept me awake all that night
With the smell and warmth of your body
Your sounds roaring in my ears

I am alone now
July is still hot
And you are gone again for eleven days
But you still keep me awake all night
Your silence now roaring in my ears

Tides

Sometimes, we journey to the coast
Wiggle our toes in wet sand
Feel the wind
Wait for the sun to rise
. . . and listen
As clumsy waves speak in code
About the sea and its love sacrifice to the moon

Bob Hinkle

Some nights, alone, outside, the breeze ruffles my hair
The heat of the day lingers in the concrete warming the
    soles of my feet
The moon shakes in ecstasy upon the water
Night sounds talk with one another in melodies and
    harmonies
I see a man treading water waving his long fingered hands
Imploring me to save him; pull him to shore so we may sit
    and talk for a while
I hear distant thunder and go inside before it rains
But I am telling my waking dream before I tell you why

The dream begins a lifetime ago in church on hundreds of
    dreary Sunday mornings
Only music makes it tolerable, but this dream is not about
    singing hymns
This is about a friend, an award-winning concert organist
    who played Carnegie Hall
Who returns to his nativity to become the organist and
    choral director
To a congregation that does not understand his kind love
Does not want to hear him testify
As his long fingers dance upon the keys with God
So late at night, when the unbelievers sit at home upon their
    couches
He calls down the God of Thunder
His testimony makes the stained glass windows shake with
    ecstasy

He leaves a side door open
I come inside; I sit, transfixed, awed and envious
For I know I can never love like this
Later, we talk about creativity, art, being different and
        never fitting in
But this, too, is not the story of my waking dream
The story I sat down to write is of a gentle man
Who befriends a lonely, angry boy
Years pass, the boy grows to be a man
His friend is arrested in the park
Where gay men leave a car door open
Hoping someone may come and visit for awhile
Forced from his church, he flees to the big city
His long fingered hands now work arranging flowers for
        a florist
I tell myself that I will go find him
Thank him for helping me survive the trauma of being
different
Tell him what his friendship meant to me.
But I waited too long
The first wave of AIDS crashes upon our shores
I hear the distant thunder

This is not about singing hymns

It Lingers

This morning, watching mist rise off the lake
No wind, the water is motionless
Clouds float above my face in a liquid mirror
I am an interloper and a voyeur
Someone who does not belong here
O' the air hangs heavy over the 'Land of Cotton'
It lingers in the streets, in the fields
In the air above still water

I was born on the banks of the Wabash
Where winds blow hard
Coming down off the Great Lakes
Like a speeding semi out of Chicago
Barreling over the plains of the Calumet
Heading south on I65 towards Indianapolis
Winds that build snow drifts in the winter
Winds that change the seasons
Winds that cool the summer heat

Yesterday, my wife came home from college
She had given a lecture on racial identity
Showing a series of photographs of people
She asked students to identify race
Some were of our grandchildren
A white student apologized for calling them black
A black student asked if she went
Out in public with our grandchildren
. . . a culture still shackled . . .
O' the air hangs heavy over the 'Land of Cotton'
It lingers in the streets, in the fields
In the air above still water

Sometimes II

Last month, Mom called me asking if I was coming home
    for Easter
Reminding me I had not driven the 700 miles since
    Christmas
And telling me three times in three different ways
How it hurts to get on her knees and plant spring flowers
And that my father forgets what he has done and
    overwatered the daffodils again
Sometimes, she makes me feel like it is my fault he is
    getting old
I wonder when will be my last time
To sit at their table so she can feed me breakfast
Food that she remembers as my favorite
Food that I now only eat at their table
Where I will listen to her tell stories
About her parents and grandparents

We drove home that Easter
I ate breakfast at their table, heard the same stories, picked
    up sticks in the yard
Pulled weeds from her flowers, watched her sing in the
    church choir
. . . and sometimes, I would sit on their couch
Searching for words to describe
My feelings of all the time she has gifted me
My mind spinning in circles
Like a dog chasing its tail
Trying to find words to sink my teeth into
But a dog never seems to catch its tail
And I never seem to find the words

II

Edge of the Woods

I used to hide at the edge of the woods among the brambles
Where no one could see me watching
Watching clouds drift
Watching shadows move
Watching field mice scurry
Watching butterflies flit
Watching willy worms crawl
Watching lovers undress
Watching — never knowing how
Never knowing who
Never knowing what
Never knowing when
Never knowing why
Never knowing if I had a right to be there
Hidden at the edge of the woods among the brambles
Where no one could see me

Fog

Watching her car disappear into the hills
He stands outside the bunker of their last stand
The haze of battle still sits heavy
Neither side took any prisoners
A thin curtain drawn across the sun
The fog covers her escape route
Mute trees stand as sentinels
Guarding her retreat

Here in this southern land
They fought to make a life together
But like the Cherokee – she melts
Into the western hills – never to return

Blue Tick Hound, or a Southern Tale

Dog on a chain
Too big for the kitchen
Humane Society said this was cruel
Took off the chain

Fenced him in the backyard
To roll in his waste
Bark at the door
. . . and dig at the gate

Gristle and Bone

Stars fill night skies
Tonight, I hope the coyotes eat my neighbor's cat
Dogs seek any handout
Deer freeze in headlights
Buzzards feast on road kill
Whores suck their living from gristle and bone
Sleepers wake from dreaming
Birds sing songs of light
City buses always come late
Unemployed or under-employed it's all the same
Homeless listen for the library lock to click open
Veterans drink coffee and talk of the good ol' days that
      never were

Voyeur

I stand outside watching the moon undress
As she walks naked past the window of the sky
On her way upstairs to lie among the stars
She wraps her bright nakedness
In a blanket of clouds and goes to bed alone

His Hands

His hands promised affection
And offered sweet gifts
She nuzzled at his shoulder
Silently asking his hands
To take her to a private place

One hand to stroke her face
One hand to gently lead her
Through the open gate

Fenced by cultural expectations
And the barbed wire of social graces
She now comes to the gate when called
Looking for handouts – seeking affection
From the hands of her butcher

To The Girl Unknown

Jamestown 1609 — The Starving Time
Rumors of cannibalism
New York Times 2013 — rumors confirmed

To the girl unknown
Whose leg they gnawed upon
What is your story?
Were you the servant girl or beloved daughter?
Were you murdered to be eaten?

What is your story?
You sailed across the ocean
Only to slowly starve
Native warriors lurking outside your door?
No Thanksgiving dinner
No Squanto
No turkey giblets with oyster dressing

Were you pretty?
Did anyone ever lust for your body
Your tender shanks of bloody flesh?
Did anyone know you dreamed
Of children suckling at your breast?
Had you eaten others before it was your turn?

Daughter of Light

Daughter of Light
You have slept through your alarm
The sun is filtering through curtains hung a lifetime ago
You must leave his warm bed — no turning back

But how do you tell someone you must leave
If they only know their own voice
When what you must say can only be said
In the language of your dreams

Let your emotions lie in shredded heaps
Upon the floor of the house of your visitation
Walk away quickly — clad only by the sun
Leave only your bare footprints in the dew of his front yard

A Letter to Miss Harvey

Dear Miss Harvey,

Sometimes, when the air grows cool and color drains from
      the trees
I know the beauty of death
. . . and I sit wondering if this is how it was to watch you
In your mother's fur coat sitting in your car with the garage
      door pulled down
As the color drained from your face and your world grew
      cold

What led you there?

You the middle child, who was never good enough for your
      father
Now the perfect suburban housewife with your prescription
      drugs, vodka martinis
Breakdowns, affairs and guilt
Your husband all too happy to goad you along

Always rebellious, you did not give the country club public
      their accident
Instead, you gently drifted off dressed in your mother's fur
      coat
In the front seat of your car with fine vodka on your breath
As the color drained from your face and your world grew
      cold.

But — but — but Anne, what if it's not that simple?

Sincerely, Al

Poem for a Friend Whose Lover Committed Suicide

I lie awake tonight
As a distant train wails out its sad goodbye
Passing through on its way to somewhere or nowhere
I know not which

Your scent is on my pillow
Alone I listen
For your midnight knock on my door
Was this only a four-year one-night stand?

I lie here waiting for your return
For you to kiss my swollen breasts
To rock me – to hold me – to help me
Through this long night

When spring comes and daylight lingers
I will plant roses by the railroad track to wave goodbye
So I may sleep or maybe love again
I know not which

A Generation of Mad Hatters

In 1961, before we knew
That mercury would make you crazy
My friend and I used to collect
Mercury from broken thermometers
And bring it for show-and-tell

At recess we would smash it
Just to watch it explode
We would collect the drops
Let it roll about in the palm of our hands
The drops would find each other and become whole

Then Viet Nam exploded on our TV screens
McNamara's lie – Johnson's Waterloo
All the thermometers were broken
We no longer knew the temperature
But we were hot as hell

Alice beckoned us through her looking glass
She fed us on magic mushrooms
While the Mad Hatter chattered on
Laughing at our madness – watching us
Chase mercury and hold it in our hands

Today, we again are invited to sit at a tea party
As the Cheshire Cat keeps grinning
We fear their madness
But still we chase mercury across the floor
Try to hold it in our hands – hoping to become whole again

Exit 141

Sunday school, rebellion, and testosterone fires
An adolescent time warp trinity beckons me
Exit 141 on the interstate that rides the side of a mountain
On my way back to where I have been
Here sits a white 150 foot cross
Shading an Adult World XXX Super Store
Across the highway from Rocket Discount Fireworks

I laugh every time I drive by – wanting to stop
But Jung screams in my ear, "Don't stop
This is a synchronicity portal of your dreaming adolescent
    self
All logic will be stripped away
You will face yourself without your David Koresh mask
Sitting naked, spouting Bible verses
A harem of concubines fawning at your feet
While your finger twitches on a detonator
Ready to blow us all to Hell"

Again, I drive by
I do not stop
. . . but one day
On my way back to where I have been
I will pull over and leap into the portal
Leaving behind my tattered Bible
A pack of matches and an unfilled Viagra prescription

Blood

Blood upon the jungle floor — blood upon the Kings of
    Ghana
Blood upon the deck of ships — blood upon the sea
Blood upon the auction block — blood upon the shackles
Blood upon the cotton bales stacked high in Charleston Bay

Blood upon the ramparts — blood upon the bayonets
Blood upon Antietam fields – blood upon the swords of
    wrath
Blood upon 600,000 graves – blood upon the rebel flag
Blood upon a band that plays sweet Dixie Land

Blood upon old money — blood upon a crow named Jim
Blood upon white sheets – blood upon a hangman's noose
Blood upon a billy club – blood upon a hotel balcony
Blood upon this nation – blood upon you and me

Estrangement

Euclid was a shy boy
Detached and introspective to a fault
Boys bullied him on the playground
And girls made fun of his clothes
Quietly passive/aggressive, he plotted revenge
Theoretically drawing lines with chalk upon their backs
Dreaming of cutting them from point A to point B

Euclid was a clever boy
Postulating the theory of parallel lines
Long thin ribbons stretching out for infinity
Separate, but dancing together
Keeping their distance – never engaging one another
He served revenge cold – one math lesson at a time
Papers covered with red X's like welts from a whip

Such is the case with our estrangement
We postulate theories to define our positions
We dance in our passive/aggressive behaviors
Living parallel lives at a safe distance
Nursing old hurts and imagining new ones
Like Euclid's revenge served cold
We dance together – yet – alone and apart

Childhood Friends

My childhood friends were numbers
We often played together
Laying flash cards out across
The living room floor like dominoes
Pairing up lonely factors for dancing partners

Later at school dancing was not allowed
We were chained in chalkboard dungeons
Whipped with postulates and theorems
Made to groveled in piles of chalk dust
Silently, calculating the end of our twelve year sentence

But some numbers were not captured
They hid inside the intersecting lines
Of window frames, the patterned holes in ceiling tiles
The prisms in light fixtures
And the lines upon my tablet

I would close my ears and laugh in silent reverie
At teachers who could not see the magic
Or remember the stories of Pythagoras
Or daydream with Newton under the apple tree
Or gaze off in space with Einstein as he rode the train

Numbers used to play with me
We played dominoes in the sunlight
We danced about the room
Laughing at the unbelievers
Who could not hear the music

Henry Miller

In the living room closet
Of my childhood home on the top shelf
Where family games were kept
Racko, Parcheesi, checkers, Password . . .
Under my father's hat was a stack Readers Digest Condensed novels
At the bottom with its spine pressed tight against the wall
I found Henry hiding with his 'Tropic of Cancer'
Dripping spoo and testosterone
No more Aesop's Fables or Bullfinch's Greek Mythology
This was why Helen launched 10,000 ships
She, the bigamist, who sat upon a foreign wall
Watching brave Hector die while Paris plowed her fields
Knowing it did not matter who won
For she would be carried home
. . . and King Menelaus would spend eternity looking for a
    field
That hadn't felt a Trojan plow

Herstory

We have white history, black history, and American history
We have European history, world history, and all kinds of
      other history
But it is only half of the story
What of herstory?

Herstory is of the mothers who bore us
Herstory is the breasts we suckled
Herstory is who dried our tears
Herstory is who was our first teacher

Herstory is being held on a pedestal
With chains forged by men
Herstory is who first found the strength to believe
While Peter denied and hid in fear

Herstory started the bus boycott
That made a Baptist minister famous
Herstory has few buildings and streets named in her honor
Herstory should be a national holiday called Rosa Parks
      Day

Ourstory is when women are no longer chattel
Ourstory is when veils no longer hide female faces from
      men
Ourstory is when mothers are valued more than warriors
Ourstory is when history is no longer writing herstory

Don't Call Me Jonah

Often, I watch the sunrise
As leviathans of the ocean skies
Breach the morning clouds
Wondering — to what city in need of prophecy do they flee
Their silver bellies full of souls?

Inside this boney prison
I beat on ribs
Make music on this bloody xylophone
. . . and sing
I did not ask to be born
I did not ask to cast my lot in life's storm
I will not cry, I will not beg
I will not grovel, I will not give prophecy
I will not seek release and vomit my soul on Ninevah's
     shore

But I will watch the sunrise
As leviathans of the ocean skies
Breach the morning clouds
Wondering — to what city in need of prophecy do they flee
Their silver bellies full of souls

III

I Only Left For Tea

We return here often
To resume mid-sentence
Our conversation upon my deck
Paisley patterned spinning backward
Then forward – narrowing and swelling into its self
Like designs upon a blanket

Is time a straight line?
Postulated geometry – point A to point B
Or maybe, it is a long and colorful ribbon that ties
Our gift of time together
Moments that are more than anniversaries
To etch upon our gravestones

You and I return here often
To resume our full-flight soaring
On communion's thermal zephyrs
What is yesterday – today – tomorrow?
I only left for tea
We return here often – wrapped in our paisley blanket
To resume mid-sentence

Grandma's Cabinet

Grandma's cabinet had an upper shelf
Where she kept a ball of string
Bits and pieces – scraps knotted together
Waiting to unwind – new needs to tether

This piece from the butcher
Wrapped around the roast
This one tied the roses blooming by the pine
      Her past rolled in her ball of twine

I have saved my memories
Recycled, binding my soul like roses
Bits and pieces – scraps knotted together
Wanting to unwind – my spirit to untether

Pink Roses

Mom called this morning
With childhood stories to tell
Stories about pink roses
And how they make her sad

How her crazy grandma lived with them
She would chase them with a butcher knife
They would hide in the chicken house
Until her father came home

When her grandma died
She was laid out upon a table in the living room
 Family and friends came throughout the night
To pay respects and to make sure she was dead

Uncle Henry's wild unwed daughter
Arrived in a shiny car with a vase of pink roses
Laid them by the body
Smiled and walked out

Prefab Cracker Boxes

Boomer baby prefab cracker boxes
Filled the prairies
Sprouting up in the middle of cornfields
Between the fairgrounds and the railroad tracks
My hometown grew a bumper crop
I lived in one

At night, I would lie awake
Listen to the lonely trains as they ran away into night
Wheels thrummed a low mantra of
. . . *come, come, come, come, come* . . .
Its sorrowful horn called
"Leave now, leave now, . . . before it's too late"

Last night, I sat up late
Listening to the lonely trains as they ran away into night
Wheels thrumming a low mantra of
. . . *come, come, come, come, come* . . .
Its sorrowful horn calling,
"Leave now, leave now, . . . before it's too late"

You came out of our bedroom
. . . and said
"Dear, it's too late, come to bed"

Singing With the Frogs

Last night, I sat upon the deck
Serenaded by frogs calling for a lover
Every size and every color
Praying for a grace – looking for a mercy
Crying, "Come my love and relieve my longing"

Often, I sit upon the deck
Praying that you will come to me
And not leave me alone until morning
Singing with the frogs and
Crying, "Come my love and relieve my longing"

Tomorrow, I will arise before the dawn
To sit upon the deck again
I will say my prayers
And listen to a few lonely frogs still
Crying, "Come my love and relieve my longing"

Stone Moss

Early light casts long shadows
The garden gate stands open
Dewy moss lies naked on the stone

Curtains drawn against the morning
We try not to wake each other
While hip to thigh eternity beckons

Prometheus

Oh, my Love, you want a warm bed
But I would give you fire
Watch the world burn around us
While you chain me to your bed, tear my flesh
Grab me by my root and shake it like a bloody giblet

Knowing this, knowing the searing
Knowing the chains and the tearing of my flesh
I would still offer you fire
Today & tomorrow & tomorrow & tomorrow . . .
Until all eternity becomes ash

Daybreak

Yellow dawn
Cracks open
Broken egg upon the edge of darkness
Songbirds sing the night to sleep

Dim Light of Expectations

In the dim light of the back bedroom
Where I grew to manhood
I left her sleeping

She calls — she is awake
She says "Wait there & sit with me for coffee"
She does not want to drink alone

It would be easy to return to where I began
Pull the blanket of family, friends and memories over my
        head
. . . and breathe the stale air of expectations to stay the same

Questions I Ask of Spring

In the Deep South, spring waits at the garden gate
Wisteria & trees intertwine
Exchanging winter grays & browns for bright blooming
        blouses
Air smells alive
Fertile earth is warm crumbling between my fingers
A handful of dust – ions in the making
Sprinkled with the birth of stars
Blood & bones of Cherokee – of European – of African
Struggling no longer, united in my hand
Fertile earth to feed future generations
Is war inevitable? – Will peace come only in clouds
From the chalk dust of Einstein's equations?
Or is peace born in a new springtime
As it enters at the gate?

Alone

Walking the pebbled path of white hue
Where birds carol in the sun
I approach along a fragrant flowered avenue
Just beyond Amelia's wrought iron gate
Where royal cedars stand guard
And olive trees circumambulate
I come — head bowed — stepping silent on the stone
Lying at the holy threshold
In prayer this seeker comes alone

Three Poems for Others

Katie

Katie, cousin I never knew
You found me on Facebook
Seeking memories you never had
Childhood cousins to play with on sunny days

Katie, daughter of my grandfather's younger brother
Swept away to California by the Great Depression
Never to return; never to meet over family dinners
We played together on sunny days 2,000 miles apart

Marci's Poem

To be effortlessly light or brilliant
How lovely is that?
Some say maybe lambent

To have a gentle glow
To flicker lightly over the surface
Luminous our friendship will grow

Jo Ellen's Gift

You send me new age music
Endless strings of ones and zeros **on silicon wafers**
    Old friends need to sit together
    Not trapped in binary code
Laughing, drinking tea, eating sugar wafers
And speaking of dreams unborn

Playing House

Growing up my sisters were always playing house
Cooking mud pies, playing dress up, nursing favorite dolls
Childhood dreams and visions longing to unfold
This is how they grew; their futures written on sheaves of
    sunlight

Today a cry for help – a broken ankle – one takes a plane
    ride south
Endless games of practice become real
Laughing – crying – bickering – lives forever joined
Two gray-haired grandmas again are playing house

Walking the Banks

River Banks

Born along the Wabash
Summers I swam naked in the creek
Lying on this river bank
The Saluda tells me secrets
"All rivers flow into the sea
. . . and you are always home"

Sycamore Tree

Your bright arms glistening – reaching for the sky
We stood alone – the sun warming our limbs
Our youthful days along the Wabash shore
Dreaming of new tomorrows

Today I walk the banks of the Congaree
Alone in pine forests with cypress and wisteria vines
The sun warms my limbs as I remember
Your bright arms glistening – reaching for the sky

40th Anniversary — Isle of Palms

. . . walking at midnight
Low tide and wet sand
Cloud blanket pulled over a naked sky
Eastern horizon curves from north to south
Ship lights hover on the edge
While white waves dance with dry land
They hum a low mantra of worlds unknown

Summer Solstice II

Laughing – standing naked under the stars
Every crevice glistened with sweat
Our love blanket fragrant beneath our feet
As the dawn tore holes into the faded fabric of the night
We pulled on threadbare jeans
No you – no me – only us

Four Haiku

We're all immigrants
Mother pushed us from her womb
"Leave and don't return"

Upon the same branch
The red rose and thorn reside
You must water both

A raging river
Will never reveal your face
Sit still and reflect

Lay down your burdens
How can you receive presents
If your hands are full?

Winter Poem

From last winter to this winter,
The difference is very noticeable

My parents are old and frail
My father is not up yet and it is after 6 a.m.

They sleep more than they are awake.

They are still in their home
Trying to take care of each other

I can't help but wonder,
Is this our last Christmas together?

Blankets

I love the peace of a snowy night
That falls as a sky tossed blanket
Over the nakedness of my town
Each flake laughing — oh, so quietly
About a myriad acts of kindness

I love the peace she brings me
Covering my shivering soul
With our quilted marriage blanket
Each fold a joy — a pain — a challenge won
Forty years and counting

Memories the threads that stitch the fabric
Covering our nakedness

Weightless

If you pray to be of service and I pray for relief
Are we guided to meet?
When you say a kind word or you bind my wounded soul
Are we the answer to our prayers?
Are we assisted by hosts of angels?
Do angels land weightless upon our thoughts
When immersed in prayer?
How would we know?

Soon

Yesterday, Dad called
He said, "All the leaves have fallen from the trees
. . . and the morning frost lies like sugar glazing upon
      the ground"
He asked, "When are you coming home?"
I said, "Soon"
He said, "It looks like it will be a cold winter"

Today, Mom called
She said, "Aunt Edna's cancer has returned
. . . and Friday the doctors will begin chemo and radiation,
      again"
She asked, "When are you coming home?"
I said, "Soon"
She said, "I have some old pictures to show you"

Once upon a time, there was a Greek god who dressed in
      beggar's clothes
On a warm day, he sat with an old couple
. . . and heard stories of their love and long life together
One cool evening, dressed in god robes
He returned, stood outside their door and gave them
The gift of dying together in their sleep

Tonight
Just for tonight
I wish I were a Greek god who dressed in beggar's clothes

Acknowledgements

First and foremost, I want to thank my wife, Carol Agnew Black, my parents, Chester and Alice Black, our children, Jasmine, Leah, Jamal, and Levin and my siblings, Barb, Kathy, Brad, Dave and Janet for allowing me to become who I am.

I have had a tempestuous relationship with school and teachers; however, I would be remiss to not thank Mrs. Luetkemeier, who never told me I was bad or made me sit in the hall, Roger Clausen, who would counsel me that I did not have to always fight and have a hate relationship with the world and Doug Paprocki and Professor John Barber who empowered, did not preach and did not talk down.

I want to acknowledge a long list of poets and writers of which these are but a few: Emily, Anne, Edna, Carl, Langston, Walt, Gwendolyn, John Dunne, George Herbert, Kahlil Gibran, the peerless Rumi, Kundera, Nin, Matthiessen Baldwin, and Steinbeck (Tom Joad, my hand is on a shovel and I got your back). Three Columbia poets, Charlene Spearen, Jerlean Noble, and Cassie Premo Steele have encouraged and guided me to opportunities, thank you.

Lastly, I must acknowledge some folks who if not for them this book would not have seen the light of day. Cindi Boiter and Dr. Bob Jolley who asked me to publish with Muddy Ford Press when publishing was not on my wish list. Ed Madden for his expert and gracious editing and for assuring me that my poetry was worth publishing. Kevin Neireiter for creating an original piece of art for the book cover and Mustapha, for photography and the video of the title poem, *I Only Left for Tea.*

About the Author

A Hoosier in the land of cotton, Al Black was born and raised in Lafayette, Indiana. He has been married 42 years to Carol Agnew Black; they have four grown children and nine grandchildren. Black was drafted and served as a Conscientious Objector during the Vietnam era, attended Ball State and Purdue Universities, and is a Baha'i. By day he has worked in various management positions and been a business owner; by night he has been an athlete, coach, community activist, and town gadfly.

Black began writing verse at age nine, but kept his poems strictly to himself. In late 2008, he moved to South Carolina so his wife could accept a job as a professor of Sociology. Unemployed for the first time and free from family and community expectations, he publicly shared his first poetry four years ago. Black considers himself a northern born Southern poet because it was here in the South that he felt free to blossom.

About the Cover Artist

Kevin Neireiter is a multi-media artist who lives in the Pacific Northwest. In his spare time he enjoys cooking, music, and nature. He has known the poet Al Black since he was 15 years old. Black was invaluable in impressing upon the artist that the world is a much bigger place than small town Indiana.

Also from Muddy Ford Press

Jasper Reads: Download
Edited by Ed Madden

To the Wren Nesting
By Kristine Hartvigsen

Buttered Biscuits: Short Stories from the South
By Cynthia Boiter

Fellow Traveler
By James McCallister

The Limelight, volume 1
Edited by Cynthia Boiter

All the In Between: My Story of Agnes
By Laurie McIntosh

Red Social: Portraits of Collaboration
By Alejandro Garcia-Lemos and Cynthia Boiter

Jasper Presents The 2nd Act Film Festival Screenplays
Edited by Wade Sellers and Cynthia Boiter

Woman Commits Suicide in Dishwasher
By Debra A. Daniel

A Sense of the Midlands
Edited by Cynthia Boiter and Ed Madden

www.ingramcontent.com/pod-product-compliance
Lightning Source LLC
Chambersburg PA
CBHW052113070526
44584CB00017B/2471